# Elves

by Grace Hansen

Abdo Kids Jumbo is an Imprint of Abdo Kids
abdobooks.com

**abdobooks.com**

Published by Abdo Kids, a division of ABDO, P.O. Box 398166, Minneapolis, Minnesota 55439.

Abdo Kids Jumbo™ is a trademark and logo of Abdo Kids.

Printed in China

052022

092022

THIS BOOK CONTAINS RECYCLED MATERIALS

Photo Credits: Alamy, Everette Collection, Getty Images, Granger Collection, Shutterstock PREMIER

Production Contributors: Teddy Borth, Jennie Forsberg, Grace Hansen
Design Contributors: Candice Keimig, Pakou Moua

Library of Congress Control Number: 2021950544

Publisher's Cataloging-in-Publication Data

Names: Hansen, Grace, author.

Title: Elves / by Grace Hansen.

Description: Minneapolis, Minnesota : Abdo Kids, 2023 | Series: World of mythical beings | Includes online resources and index.

Identifiers: ISBN 9781098261894 (lib. bdg.) | ISBN 9781098262730 (ebook) | ISBN 9781098263157 (Read-to-Me ebook)

Subjects: LCSH: Elves--Juvenile literature. | Mythical animals--Juvenile literature. | Folklore--Juvenile literature. | Legends--Juvenile literature.

Classification: DDC 398.21--dc23

# Table of Contents

# Myth of the Elf

Elves are special kinds of **fairies**. They have pointed ears. They mainly appear in the **folklore** of northern Europe.

## Scandinavian Elves

When people think of elves, two opposite beings can come to mind. One is human-sized and **slender**. Its skin shimmers like the sun. It can live for hundreds of years.

These kinds of elves often appear in **Scandinavian mythology**. They can be both helpful and harmful toward humans.

**Norse** tales tell of a land of elves. The land is close to the gods. Other myths say that elves lived in kingdoms. These kingdoms could be in forests, meadows, or trees.

## Other Elves

The other type of elves are tiny beings. They can be happy and kind creatures. They like to help with human chores.

Others are dark and mean. They steal from people. In some stories, tiny elves use magic for bad and to cause illnesses.

In German mythology, elves sat on sleeping people's chests. They caused bad dreams. A German word for nightmare, *alpdrücken*, means "elf pressure."

Some stories warned of elves stealing human babies. The elves replaced the young children with **changelings**.

## Elves Today

Elves are still well-known creatures today. But most are shown as happy and very helpful. Some work in trees making cookies. Others build toys at the North Pole.

from
Santa

# Modern Elves based on Mythology

**Dobby**
*Harry Potter* series

- Helpful
- Has magical abilities
- Does chores for humans

**Legolas**
*The Lord of the Rings*

- From the Woodland Realm of a great, dark forest
- Has special abilities
- Can only die in battle
- Has skin that shines

**Puck**
Shakespeare's *A Midsummer Night's Dream*

- Good hearted and playful
- Has magical abilities
- Capable of cruel tricks

# Glossary

**changeling** – a strange child believed to be secretly swapped by fairies or elves for the parents' real child as a baby.

**fairy** – a type of mythical being found in the folklore of many European cultures. Fairies are often described as human in appearance and having magical powers.

**folklore** – the stories and ways of a group of people from a certain place or country.

**Norse** – of or having to do with Scandinavia.

**Scandinavian mythology** – the folklore of Denmark, Norway, Sweden, Iceland, and the Faroe Islands. It shares common roots with folklore from other European countries.

**slender** – slim or thin.

# Index